WePROV

The Monologue Collection, Volume III

Published by Akilah Logan, 2018

While every precaution has been taken in the preparation of this book, the publisher assumes no responsibility for errors or omissions, or for damages resulting from the use of the information contained herein.

INPROV

First edition. July 25, 2018.

ISBN: 978-0-692-17056-4

Copyright © 2018 Akilah Logan.

Written by Akilah Logan.

OPEN YOUR HEART, OPEN YOU MIND TO THE ENDLESS POSSIBILITIES THAT LAY IN FRONT OF YOU…

FOREWORD

So many actors struggle with the idea of working a 9 to 5 to support themselves while pursuing their dreams. *"TO BE OR NOT TO BE"* an Actor?! That is the question. Here's the answer. If you are truly S.E.R.I.O.U.S about pursuing your dreams then it's important to support your dreams until your dreams can support you. So, with that said...Create a new way of thinking, create a new way of living, create a new way of being. I always encourage actors to ask three important questions when breaking down their scenes, and I strongly believe this applies to real life...to real people, to everyone.

Question #1: What Do I Want?
Question #2: What's Stopping Me From Getting What I Want?
Question #3: Who Am I?

Once you can answer these questions, you will solve your problem but only if you are truly honest with yourself.

Akilah and I met at my One On One Acting Class. We would meet once per week in my New Jersey office in Downtown Newark. Each week we would dive into Scene Work, Character Work and Emotional Work. We would apply my 3 rules to the monologue assigned the week before and each week it would be an eye-opening experience as she discovers the best way to utilize her acting tools. I always end each class with Akilah by saying "do you have any questions regarding our session?" She sometimes hesitates before she speaks but this one particular night she said she was struggling with moving, making money and being true to herself.

So, I asked her my three favorite questions, "What Do You Really Want? What's Stopping You From Getting What You Want? and Who Are You?" By the time we finished answering all three questions she was on the path to success.

Here's the deal, we are all given a Special Skill, Talent, A Gift... however you want to word it, whatever "it" is. It's there and here's how you recognize it. It's the first thing you think about when you wake up in the morning. It's the last thing you think about before you go to bed. It's the thing that wakes you up out of your sleep at night. It's your PASSION. And its inside of you waiting to be unleashed. So, let it out and you can turn your dreams into a reality and that salary into a salary.

During our talk, I said to Akilah, "If you have a special skill or a hidden talent. Find a way to make money doing it. If you think it, Ink it. Create a plan and stick to it."

I discovered she's an amazing writer and a good story teller and as you know by now she's written monologue books for aspiring actors and actresses. This will allow her to support her dreams until her dreams can support her. Dream Big.

Wendy Mckenzie
Acting Coach / Creative Director

Table of Contents

IS THAT WHAT YOU REALLY WANT? 13
I THINK I DO 19
MAKE BELIEVE 27
TRANSFERENCE OF POWER 30
ONE LIFE? 41
ARE YOU REALLY FOR ME? 47
WHAT YOU DON'T SEE 52
THY WILL BE DONE 59
CUT THE CHORD 63
FORGIVENESS DOES NOT EQUAL ACCEPTANCE 73
RANSOM FOR TRUTH 80
THE SWITCHEROO 85
LIKE A WHIRLWIND 92
GAMES ARE TOO STRONG 99
MAN OF THE HOUSE 105
I SEE YOU LOUD AND CLEAR 111
FINISH WHAT YOU STARTED 117
THE CULPRIT 122
WHAT ABOUT ME? 126
RELIGIOUS SECRETS 133
HIDDEN LOVE, THAT'S TRUE 141
LOVE OF DRAMA 146
YOU THINK YOU WANT THIS 151
LOVERS OVER FRIENDS 159

IS THAT WHAT YOU REALLY WANT?

Diana:
So, this is what you wanted?

Monroe:
What do you mean?

Diana:
For me to be next to you. All the time. Contributing to our household. You know, the wife duties I need to do.

Monroe:
Ok, I think you're taking this a little too serious?

Diana:
Serious? You think? According to you, I work too much. I don't spend enough time with the family. Meaning you and Baron, THE DOG. So, I took it upon myself to be what YOU want me to be.
A wife.

Monroe:
Diana, you're making this disagreement more than what we previously discussed. All I said, I wanted to see you more, hang out more. Was that too hard to ask?

Diana:
You weren't saying all this when you were working.
When Noland and Terrence would come over…EVERY DAY and spend hours over here, I didn't hear not one peep out of you. You barely noticed that I wasn't here. Did you even know my name?

Monroe:
What are you crazy?! Of course, I noticed. I was going through some hard times. I was the one that got laid off remember? Couldn't find another job for 2 straight months…and counting. Worked for a company gave all my time, all my energy…MY BEST IDEAS and they turn around use them without me. I just needed my brothers to get me through.

Diana:
You needed your brothers? Well what am I here for? I thought you pledged your life to me? I thought you told ME for richer or poorer till death do us part? I didn't know you married your "brothers" too?!

Monroe:
That's not what I meant. I just needed them to help me figure out my next steps.

Diana:
Those next steps should have been discussed with me.

Monroe:
D, you don't know what it's like to be a man, to promise to take care of someone for the rest of your life. Then out of nowhere you get laid off and your wife is working doing the job I'm supposed to do.

Diana:
I am in no way, doing your job. I am doing my job. To be your helpmeet. You didn't marry some lazy woman who didn't know how to take care of herself AND her family. I didn't ask you to take care of me either. I asked you to work with me to build a future that couldn't be done alone. This unnecessary pressure is something that YOU put on yourself, not me.

Monroe:
So, then what do you suggest I do then? Huh? Work at McDonald's till my next job?

Diana:
I don't understand why you need a job? Why don't you start a business?

Monroe:
Because we can't afford it.

Diana:
Who says?

Monroe:
I see the bills.

Diana:
You mean the bills you ran up and I already paid off because I got us bills? Those?

Monroe:
Come on Diana, you know I was depressed.

Diana:
Yea and you ran off to your "brothers". Wasn't realizing that I, your wife, your best friend was holding us down. Now all of a sudden, you're intimidated by me working like this wasn't who you married. When I am EXACTLY who you married. An independent woman that handles her business. I didn't need you for money, my self-esteem, or my worth. You knew I wasn't some save me kind of woman but you still married me. And you expect me to change because you're questioning your manhood just because I'm working?! Nah.

Monroe:
See, that's why I went to them. Cause you don't understand.

Diana:
No, what I don't understand is this level of insecurity that you have never showed me. Now I'm feeling bamboozled.

Monroe:
I thought you were liked that just because you were single. I thought you would fall back because we're married now. There's no need for you to be independent because I'm here!

Diana:
In who's world?! Are we building together or are you building and I have to sit here and accept it?

Monroe:
Clearly, we have two different views on what we need.

Diana:
CLEARLY.

I THINK I DO

Brian:
Can we talk for a second?

Hailey:
Sure, I have a meeting in a little bit but I have time.

Brian:
Over the past year, we've been working together. We have the best numbers. We talk about everything. All in all, we've grown pretty close, wouldn't you say?

Hailey:
Um, I would. I mean let's also be clear that you didn't make it easy for me either.

Brian:
What do you mean?

Hailey:
I see someone doesn't remember how rude you were to me in the beginning. I even overheard that you didn't think I earned my position to, remember that?

Brian:
Hmmm…nope.

Hailey:
I didn't think you would.

Brian:

Well anyway, aside from that I think you're a special woman and this company would be nothing without you…I would be nothing without you.

Hailey:
Brian, what are you talking about?

Brian:
I think I'm falling in love with you.

Hailey:
I'm sorry, excuse me?

Brian:
I'm falling in love with you.

Hailey:
Brian are you joking? You're joking.

Brian:
I'm serious. I don't know when but I started realizing that I wanted to be around you more. I don't know. I mean-

Hailey:
Ok, you don't know if you're falling in love with me or you don't know when it happened?

Brian:
I don't know when it happened.

Hailey:
I can tell you when it happened, the night you stayed over my house, which was a mistake.

Brian:
A mistake? We were working on the Williams Project.

Hailey:
I know. We stopped working at 10pm. You didn't go home.

Brian:
I know.

Hailey:
Didn't we drink that night too?

Brian:
Only a little bit.

Hailey:
WE WOKE UP TOGETHER…SIDE BY SIDE. Brian.

Brian:
But nothing happened.

Hailey:
Are you sure? You don't know that. Neither of us remember.

Brian:
Ok, ok…slow down.

Hailey:
Slow down? Slow down? You drop this bomb that you THINK you're falling in love with me. You do remember I have a man, right? The only reason why I've ignored the subject is because I'm not ruining my relationship over this. It's bad enough I don't remember what did or did not happen that night.

Brian:
Are you gonna act like you don't feel the same way?
Look me in the eye and tell me I'm wrong.

Hailey:
I can't feel the same way. Regardless of what of my heart says. NO. It's too complicated.

Brian:
How? I'm telling you I think I'm falling in love with you, that's not enough to try?

Hailey:
Try what? I'm not some jacket that you try on to see if you like it or not or some pair of sneakers you get to walk around in to see if it's a good fit. You don't FALL in love, it's a choice. You're ready to ruin

my relationship all because you wanna try! I'm not trying NOTHING with you.

Brian:
Hailey, you haven't told me that I'm wrong.

Hailey:
I can do this right now.

Brian:
Well when? I know we have a chance. You know we have a chance. Yea, I'm scared but so what. I love you. I'm IN love with you.

Hailey:
Brian, I'm engaged.

Brian:
What? When? Where's the ring?

Hailey:
It just happened ok. It's too late.

Brian:
(passionately kisses Hailey)
Are you sure?

Hailey:
Sigh.

MAKE BELIEVE

Tasha:
Good Morning! How did you sleep? I slept like a pure baby snuggled in the womb.
Ok, maybe that's a little too dramatic but fully rested is definitely an understatement.
Travis. Travis. Are you paying attention to me?

Travis:
I can't do this.

Tasha:
Can't do what?

Travis:
This. Us.

Tasha:
Oh gosh, you're on this again. What's the matter now?

Travis:
You, Me. This whole fairy tale life we faked.

Tasha:
Look, we have been through this before. I know you don't think you can go through with this but you have to. We have no choice.

Travis:
We can go to the police.

Tasha:
And tell them what? You killed someone in self-defense? You're black, Travis. It's not gonna end well for you.

Travis:
It has to. I can't keep going on lying. Telling everyone we're happy and in love. I don't even know you.

Tasha:
Travis, we've been over this. You know me, ok. You came to the coffee shop I worked at every day. We've had countless conversations about politics and music. Come on you have to remember.

Travis:
No, I don't.

Tasha:
Ok, you used to get a double espresso with mint. I would tell you that's waaay too much coffee and mint tea was better.

Travis:
Look, the only thing I remember is seeing you while I was in line. Talked with you a couple of times. You're the one who told me about your abusive boyfriend and how he would stalk you at your job.

Tasha:
And you helped me get rid of him.

Travis:
It was self-defense.

Tasha:
Who's gonna believe that? The cops? The media? You see every day how they portray black men. You're already guilty. I know this isn't ideal and I appreciate how stepped in and helped me. The least I can do is look out for you. How do you think that would make me feel? The man that killed my abusive boyfriend is in jail because of me? I can't do it!

Travis:
This is more than what I bargained for. This was supposed to be a temporary thing. Until the investigation blew over. Somehow, you've convinced yourself that this is your life and it's not.

Tasha:
Well, would it be so bad? I mean, we have a great house. Great neighbors. No one knows us, we're not on the news. You've got to see this as a good thing.

Travis:
I gotta go think. When I get back, we're gonna have a solution. Somebody is gonna hear this.

(makes a phone call)
Tasha:
Hey, he's getting restless. I think he's going to bail. Baby, I know, I know. I'm trying. He doesn't remember. He thinks you're dead. You need to figure something out because I can't keep him hostage too long.

TRANSFERENCE OF POWER

Darrell:
Where have you been?

Tina:
I ran out with my friends, I told you remember?

Darrell:
Yea, you told me you'd be home at 10…it's now 1? So, I'm gonna ask you again. Where have you been?

Tina:
Babe, we just lost track of time.

Darrell:
You couldn't call me and ask me to stay out longer? What if I had something planned for you? I would've wasted my time.

Tina:
Ok, D. I'm sorry. Next time I'll ask you.

Darrell:
Next time, oh there won't be a next time.

Tina:
What? Excuse me?

Darrell:
You heard me. You out there being reckless with those single friends of yours not taking into consideration that you have a man at home. They probably told you to leave me.

Tina:
Babe, it's really not that serious, we went to the movies and went to dinner. We would up at this lounge for a couple of drinks then I came home. What is wrong with you?

Darrell:
What's wrong with me? What's wrong with you? You could've been killed out there.

Tina:
But I wasn't. I'm home. I'm safe with you. Now, let's just go to bed. I'm tired.

Darrell:
I-I can't deal with this. Give me your phone.

Tina:
For what?

Darrell:
I think you should find some new friends. I'll hold you phone for you.

Tina:
Darrell, I am not giving you my phone. This is ridiculous.

Darrell:
Are you hiding something from you?

Tina:
What? No. I'm just not giving you my phone.

Darrell:
Give me the phone Tina!

Tina:
No! You're acting crazy, I'm going to bed!

(Darrell follows her and tries to grab her phone and tussle a little bit. In the midst of the tussle, Darrell grabs Tina's arm and slaps hard to the point she falls to the ground.

Darrell:
I'm, I'm sorry.

Tina:
What the hell Darrell!

Darrell:
I didn't mean it, I love you Tina. I just worry about you all the time.

Tina:
You slapped me...IN THE FACE.

Darrell:
I know, I won't do it again. You know I'm protective of you. I can't trust that anyone else will watch out for you, especially the way I do. What if you get robbed or raped? Or worst die? I couldn't forgive myself!! You might as well kill me too!

Tina:
It's ok, Darrell. It's ok.

Darrell:
Just the thought of some other man touching you drives me crazy. I need you here with me always!

Tina:
Darrell, you need to calm down.

Darrell:
None of your friends like me. They're just mad they don't have man that looks after them. That's why they're all bitter.

Tina:
I know. Listen to me. I love you, I'm not going anywhere.

Darrell:
But they told you to leave me, didn't they?

Tina:
It doesn't matter what anyone says. I'm not going anywhere. I'm here with you.

Darrell:
I love you Tina. I love you like I have never loved before. I don't want to imagine my life without you. Do you mind making some soup? I don't feel well.

Tina:
Sure, I'm gonna get some ice for my cheek.

Darrell:
I love you Tina.

Tina:
I love you too.

ONE LIFE?

Crystal:
Are we really doing this?

Tony:
Yea.

Crystal:
I'm scared.

Tony:
I know.

Crystal:
What if it doesn't work?

Tony:
As long as we're together. It doesn't matter.

Crystal:
Where are the other two? They just left?!

Tony:
We can't worry about them. It's just me and you. Both of us won't
make it out together.
We have to go separately.

Crystal:
How will I know you're safe?

Tony:
You won't. But I will find you. Right now, we need to get you out of
here.

Crystal:
I'm not leaving you!

Tony:
You have to! Both of us can't get caught. You have to run Crys!

Crystal:
It wasn't supposed to happen like this. In and out!

Tony:
Can't fix it now. Just gotta roll with it. Chin up. You hear me? Don't look back. I will find you. Do you remember the directions I gave you?

Crystal:
Two lefts, One right, One left and around the corner.

Tony:
Right. Remember, don't look back.

Police 1:
We have you surrounded! Come out with your hands up! There's no way out.

Crystal:
I can't, I can't.

Tony:
Crystal, look at me. You have to run.

Crystal:
I love you.

Tony:
I love you too.

(Crystal runs off, Tony makes sure he's not followed and walks out an opposite way.)

Sergeant Lewis:
Does she suspect anything?

Tony:
No. How long do I have to keep doing this?

Sergeant Lewis:
Until I say so.

ARE YOU REALLY FOR ME?

Karen:
Thank you for having me. I think it's time for me to take my seat permanently on the board. My parents have built this company from the ground up and I want to make sure that I am doing all that I can to ensure their policies and infrastructure remain the same.

Wayne:
With all due respect, Karen, while you were travelling all over the world backpacking and hiking wherever your heart desired, we have been keeping this company afloat.

Karen:
I understand that and I thank you-

Wayne:
Moreover, there are hundreds of policies and procedures that you have not been made aware of. It would take more time then I believe you are willing to give for you to comprehend them.

Karen:
With all due respect Wayne, my parents wanted me to take over the company. I'm doing just that.

Wayne:
I say wait a couple of years, take your time learning the policies and when we feel that you are ready, we will be happy to follow.

Karen:
Wayne-

Wayne:
Don't worry Karen, we'll take it from here. The company basically runs itself at this point.

Karen:
I understand that, however, I am fully capable of picking up where my parents left off.

Wayne:
I disagree.

Karen:
What do you mean? I can handle this.

Wayne:
Why would you? Your parents put us "the board" in place to make sure this company runs after their death. I'm sure there's something else you'd rather be doing.

Karen:
I-I

Wayne:
Don't worry. As stated, we'll look over the company until you are absolutely ready to take over.

Karen:
Thank you so much Wayne, for acting as my father reincarnated. Fortunately for you, I have had the help of my assistant to get me up to date with the policies that my family have put in place. Now in terms of "handing" the company over to me, you will see in the Appendix where it states that as long as there is a blood relative remaining, the company and its affiliates will be rendered to said person. That sir is me. So, should you desire to remain employed here, ALL decisions will be made, by me. Is that clear?

Wayne:
Sure.

(Change of pace)
Karen:
Will we have any more trouble out of you?

Wayne:
I don't know, you tell me?

Karen:
As long as you know who the boss is. I'm fine.

Wayne:
I'm pretty sure you KNOW who the boss is.

Karen:
Look, are you by my side or not? You know the board is going to watch everything that I do. Our relationship cannot cause any additional problems.

Wayne:
Why would it? I only acted that way so they wouldn't catch on.

Karen:
Could've fooled me? You looked a little too serious.

Wayne:
Well it worked, right? Come on, don't worry. I got you.

Karen:
Hmmm.

WHAT YOU DON'T SEE

Nikki:
Roses are red, Violets are- whatever. He told me, Jordan. He told me that he loved me.

Jordan:
I know. I know.

Nikki:
Why did he have to lie? I did everything for him. I WAS the prefect girlfriend. I supported his dreams, encouraged him when EVERYBODY told him not to start his business. When they told him it was a stupid idea and he almost gave up. Now look at him!

Jordan:
He was under a lot of pressure, Nik.

Nikki:
Are you really excusing what he did?

Jordan:
No, not at all. I'm saying that some men succumb to temptation and success. Whatever that means to them.

Nikki:
So dumping me after you got some money AND after you proposed to me…IN PUBLIC?! I'm supposed to understand that? That doesn't make sense.

Jordan:
I know. I'm just trying to help.

Nikki:
Well you're not. I just don't understand. I never pressured him about anything. He wanted to get married. I let my guard down and now look at me.

Jordan:
You're still beautiful.

Nikki:
Doesn't mean anything when the man you love totally dissed you.

Jordan:
Look at it this way, he wasn't right for you. You're better without him. His lost.

Nikki:
You're such a dope friend. Why are all the good ones gay?
Jordan:
Who's gay?

Nikki:
You?

Jordan:
Who said so?

Nikki:
Wait, you're not gay?

Jordan:
How did you think I was?

Nikki:
Well, I mean you never brought a date around or talked about anyone.

Jordan:
That's because you talked for the both of us. You do realize you have a lot of drama.

Nikki:
Ok, wait. You listen to what I say and we actually talk!

Jordan:
Nikki, you're being dumb. That's what friends do.

Nikki:
Wait, you've never tried to come on to me and I've worn some scandalous outfits in front of you.

Jordan:
And? Not every man wants to jump on you. So that's why you thought I was gay? Because I didn't harass you like every other dude? You're buggin.

Nikki:
You sat here and became one of my closest friends. Why?

Jordan:
What?! Because you're a cool person. You have way too much drama for me but you cool.

Nikki:
I wish I would've met you before Steve.

Jordan:
You did.

Nikki:
Wait, I did? When?

Jordan:
At the Suka Lounge. We had a couple of mutual friends, Funny thing, I was actually going to approach you.

Nikki:
Why didn't you?

Jordan:
Nikki, you weren't looking anywhere near my direction. You thought I was gay remember?

Nikki:
Noooo! But if you approached me, maybe it would've been different.

Jordan:
I doubt it. You were already up on some other dude.

Nikki:
Well, what do we do now?

Jordan:
We stay friends.

Nikki:
I mean-

Jordan:
Oh, you mean you and me.
No. we're just friends. Besides. I have a girlfriend.

THY WILL BE DONE

Barry:
I can't believe I only have 2 more days with you. This isn't fair.

Lisa:
I know, we just have to cherish what's left of what we have.

Barry:
I don't want you to leave me. What am I gonna do?

Lisa:
You're going to live. You're going to move on.

Barry:
Why?

Lisa:
Because I said so. Mourn but not forever. Promise me, B.

Barry:
I can't promise you. You are the love of my life. I searched long and hard for you. 10 years!
10 years of making mistakes. Praying for direction to find you. My soulmate. Now God wants to take you away from me. Why?

Lisa:
I don't know. There has to be a bigger plan. You've made the last year of my life feel so fulfilled. More than I could ever imagined. I can rest knowing what true love is. You could have left me but you didn't. God will reward you for that.

Barry:
He rewarded me when I met you.

Lisa:
Barry, you will love again. You have to love again. Just think, you get to have 2 soulmates.

Barry:
That's not funny.

Lisa:
It is to me.

Barry:
You prepared for this. I couldn't even try to.

Lisa:
I've been living with this all my life.

Barry:
But I prayed. I prayed for God to heal you!

Lisa:
And He still can! But if He doesn't. Don't blame Him. There is a bigger plan.

Barry:
Tell me that bigger plan! What kind of God would allow us to finally meet and then give us a year? What happened to a lifetime?

Lisa:
Barry, this year felt like a lifetime. Do you know the few relationships I had never spanned more than 3 months? It was too much for them. You stayed.

Barry:
Because I love you and I was hoping that God would heal you.

Lisa:
If God decides to send me home. It's for the best. Sometimes we don't get what we want because it's not in His plan. I know that's a hard pill to swallow. We have to accept it.

Barry:
You do. I don't.

Lisa:
Don't base your walk on what you don't get. Appreciate what you do get.

Barry:
What about our children? What am I supposed to tell them?

Lisa:
Tell them that I spent a wonderful year with the man that I love and I that I'll always love them. Barry, you don't have to take care of them. They were my children. I've already made arrangements.

Barry:
Who do you think is going to raise them? Your parents? They were my children for a year, I'm not letting them go. Why haven't we talked about this?

Lisa:
I wasn't going to burden you with the aftermath of my decisions once I'm gone.

Barry:
I can't believe we're having this conversation now. Those are our children. I'm raising them.

Lisa:
I love you Barry. I never meant to hurt you or leave you. I wanted to live for you. I wanted to grow old with you. I'm sorry.

Barry:
Let's just do one more prayer. Can we?

Lisa:
Together?

Barry:
Of course.

Lisa and Barry:
Our Father, who are in heaven. Hallowed be thy name…

Barry:
Thy kingdom come, thy will be done. On earth as it is in heaven.
Lisa! Lisa!! Nurse! Help!!
Please come back.

CUT THE CHORD

Phone rings.

Sam:
Hello? Hi, mom. It's 5:45am. Are you okay? Yes ma'am. I will be there at 9. Ok. Good morning too.

(8:00 am)
Beth:
Good Morning, sweetheart.

Sam:
Good Morning.

Beth:
Are you ready for this weekend?

Sam:
This weekend?

Beth:
Yes. Our cabin weekend that we had to push back because your mother had to have you drive her to her doctor's appointments.

Sam:
OH! Yea. That weekend. I can't do it.

Beth:
Why now? I mean, forget that I had to switch my schedule. Change meetings for this weekend. I'm sure she needs something again, so what is it?

Sam:
She needs me to fix a couple of cabinets in the kitchen.

Beth:
Sam. Do you know how to fix cabinets?

Sam:
I'm pretty handy.

Beth:
Since when?

Sam:
I'll be fine. I won't be long. Make sure everything is packed and we'll leave at 1.

Beth:
Okay.

(6 hours later)

Sam:
Hey babe, you ready?

Beth:
Yea. I was ready 5 hours ago. Where have you been?!

Sam:
It took me a little longer than expected. I tightened the hinges on the cabinets which I wound up making a mess. Took a while to clean up. Mom made some food. Here's a plate for you.

Beth:
You know your mother doesn't like me. I don't know how you don't see that.

Sam:
Beth, she made you a plate of food because she felt bad.

Beth:
Sam. Look at this plate. What's in it? Pork.

Sam:
Pork.

Beth:
She knows I don't eat pork. And why are there pecans on this pie when SHE KNOWS I'M ALLERGIC TO PECANS?!

Sam:
Ok. I know she's not particularly fond of you.

Beth:
Fond of me?! She's TRYING TO KILL ME. You know. It's all because of that girl, Cynthia. She never wanted me with you. It didn't matter what that girl did to you.

Sam:
But I'm with you. Doesn't that say anything?

Beth:
How can it when she has NO PROBLEM ruining our plans. Just to get her point across.
And you let her! Over and over again.

Sam:
Well what would you have me do? Huh? My father isn't around to be there for her. My brother barely comes around. I'm all she has.

Beth:
She knows that and uses it to guilt you. You are not her man. Be her son. I know she's a lot. I grew up with y'all remember? I know her. If you allow her to run your life and run me out-

Sam:
You're leaving me?!?!

Beth:
No, but she's really trying to x me out and you're letting her.

Sam:
I'm the only person that can take care of her. I'm the one that has the money and time. You know, all I wanted was to be able to take care of her so she doesn't have to struggle.

Beth:
But you have no boundaries. It's that simple. Last time I checked, you're not going to bed with your mother. If it was up to her, you'd be living in your room-FOREVER. (Pause) I'm stuck on the fact that this woman is trying to kill me and you don't care.

Sam:
I do care! I'm sure it wasn't on purpose.

Beth:
Right. And I'm an astronaut.

Sam:
Look, Enough with all of this. I'm really to go, are you?

Beth:
Let's go then. I'm waiting on you! (jokingly)

The phone rings…it's his mom.

FORGIVENESS DOES NOT EQUAL ACCEPTANCE

Jason:
Melanie?

Melanie:
Jason.

Jason:
How are you? Long time no see?

Melanie.
Sigh. I'm fine

Jason:
Wait, I'm glad I ran into you.

Melanie:
I'm not.

Jason:
Look, who knows when I'll see you again. I wanna say I'm sorry.

Melanie:
For what?

Jason:
Leading you on.

Melanie:
Is that what you call it? Leading me on?

Jason:
I mean, we were always going to be friends. I just-

Melanie:
Took up all of my time and energy. Then you left as if I wasn't needed anymore.

Jason:
Mel, I was getting into a new relationship. What would it look like if we still talked?

Melanie:
IF WE WERE JUST FRIENDS IT WOULD HAVE BEEN JUST THAT.

Jason:
We talked all the time. It would've been weird to talk to you any less. I was used to talking to you every day. I'm sure it felt weird not talking to me.

Melanie:
Actually, it felt great. I was able to get work done. Without having to divide my time with a non-boyfriend.

Jason:
Come on, Mel. You know it would've been weird.

Melanie:
See what you fail to realize is that if we remained plutonic from the beginning this would have never been an issue. You messed up a really good friendship because YOU are a confused man, literally. You treated me like I was your girl because you were lonely.

Jason:
But-

Melanie:
Yea you did. No need to lie or fake it. It's the truth. You then tried to make me feel like I was the crazy jealous one, when it was you all along. Now that's some true acting. You deserve an Oscar.

Jason:
I tried to call you, to see how you were doing.

Melanie:
I know. I changed that number. When I'm done, I'm done. There wasn't a need to communicate any further. I saw exactly how you were.

Jason:
I had some time to think and I know that I was wrong. I took advantage of you and I'm sorry. I didn't expect you to be that cool. We liked a lot of the same things. I just didn't know how to handle it.

Melanie:
Are you serious? You ruined a friendship because you couldn't handle us liking the same stuff? Isn't that what you told me about your relationship? That you guys have a lot in common. It happened so naturally? You're a piece of work. I can't believe I wasted good friendship on you.

Jason:
Do you at least accept my apology?

Melanie:
Why? To ease your conscience? You're late. I forgave you a long time ago. That's why I'm completely fine and I haven't bust your face up against a brick wall.

Jason:
I hope that we can be cordial. I know asking for more would be-

Melanie:
Completely and entirely selfish and ridiculous on your part. Look. I don't hold any grudges towards you. At the very same time, I don't trust a word that comes out of your mouth. So, whatever penance or acceptance you're looking for? Go find it somewhere else. Because this…you and I…this friendship, is dead.

Jason:
Sigh (and stares)

RANSOM FOR TRUTH

Tamara:
Hello? Hello? Who is this? What do you want?

Keith:
Tamara, what's wrong?

Tamara:
Someone has KJ.

Keith:
What?

Tamara:
Someone has KJ.

Keith:
What did they say?

Tamara:
They want 2 million dollars and something else.

Keith:
What else?

Tamara:
They didn't say.

Keith:
What? Tamara. Who- what is going on here?!

Tamara:
I don't know Keith. I want my baby!

Keith:
We have to call the police!

Tamara:
They said no police or they'll kill him.

Keith:
Some stranger expects us to drop them 2 million or what?

Tamara:
We'll never see him again.
Keith:
Ok, calm down. Let's think.

Tamara:
That is the last thing I can do! A stranger has my baby and I can't protect him!

Keith:
I know T. We will figure this out.
(Beat. Phone rings)
Hold on. Let me get it. Hello? Who is this? Where is my s-?

Tamara:
Keith, what's wrong? What are they saying?

Keith:
Is KJ my son?

Tamara:
What? Of course he's your son, why would you ask me that?

Keith:
I'm gonna ask you one more time. Tamara, Is KJ my son? Because these people know more about our lives than I can imagine. I find it very interesting

Tamara:
Why are listening to the person who has our son?! This is crazy!

Keith:
IS KJ MY SON?!

Tamara:
No.

Keith:
Who's the father? Lance.

Tamara is silent.

Keith:
ANSWER ME!

Tamara:
YES! I'm sorry. I'm sorry. You and I were separated when it happened. And I stopped it immediately when we got back together and I got pregnant. When Lance died, I didn't think knowing who the father was meant anything because I just wanted you!

Keith:
For 5 years. I've been raising your dead boyfriend's son as my own! You didn't give me the chance to figure this out.

Tamara:
You would've left me!

Keith:
How do you know?!! I guess we'll never know now, huh?!

Tamara:
I'm sorry but they still have KJ!

Keith:
I suggest you give them that 2 million.

Tamara:
Where are you going?!

Keith:
Away from you!

Tamara:
(Sobs uncontrollably.)

THE SWITCHEROO

Lana:
Hey babe.

Terrell:
Hey, how was your day?

Lana:
It was pretty good. Completed most of the work I needed to do. Closed some deals. Stressful but fine. How was your day?

Terrell:
I got stopped by the cops.

Lana:
Are you ok?

Terrell:
What did you think?

Lana:
Terrell, I just asked. What happened?

Terrell:
I went into the gas station to pay for my gas. Everything was fine. Pumped my gas. Pulled out and saw the cop following me. I crossed the light, looked in my rearview mirror and saw the lights. He asked for my license and registration. Then asked me was this my car. You know I'm pretty cool with most of the cops around here.

Lana:
Well he let you go, at least.

Terrell:
He told me to stay in the car, Lana. Next thing I know, there were 3 additional cop cars that came up.

Lana:
What did he stop you for?

Terrell:
He said this car was "supposed" to have been called as stolen.

Lana:
I can't believe this happened to you! The police around here have always been pretty respectful to us. Are you sure nothing else happened.

Terrell:
Am I sure nothing else happened? I am a black man living in the suburbs. That's enough.

Lana:
I just don't see them harassing you without probable cause.

Terrell:
Are you defending the actions of the police? He stared me dead in my face at the gas station. Waited till I drove off to stop me. All I needed was to make one wrong move and I would've been shot.

Lana:
You don't think they were just being careful to NOT catch the wrong person?

Terrell:
Lana, are you living up under a rock?

Lana:
Terrell, you don't have to be rude. I'm just trying to understand.

Terrell:
Understand this. ME, a black man lives in this neighborhood and driving what I drive already sets up red flags to cops. Cause according to them, I'm not smart enough or proper enough to have what I have.

Lana:
They never did that when I was around. I'm never bothered when I use your car.

Terrell:
It's not about you. You're the right color.

Lana:
Why does it have to be about race? Why can't it just be the cops were dumb and overzealous?

Terrell:
I can't believe we're having this conversation. I'm sitting here defending myself to a woman that it completely oblivious to the outside world!

Lana:
That is completely out of order! I understand what's going on in the world. I know that the police are targeting black men. I just want to make sure that you didn't do anything unintentionally.

Terrell:
You know, my mother was right about you!
Lana:
Excuse me?

Terrell:
As beautiful of person you are, you will never understand the world that I live in. The world I have to be on defense. The world that tells me to be a good boy and the cops won't bother you! My life could have been over and you're defending those racists cops than your own man! Do you even believe that racism exists?!

Lana:
Of course I believe that racism exists. When I look at you, I don't see color. I see a brilliant man that's changing the world.

Terrell:
And there lies our problem. How have we never talked about this? As far as I'm concerned, if you don't see color, you're ignoring the differences that we have that made our relationship and who we are special.
The you don't see color bullcrap is combining all of us into one pot-

Lana:
Is that such a bad thing? I mean out differences our what keeps us segregated. If we saw ourselves as one race and didn't focus on our differences, maybe that's how we can affect change in ourselves and community. I don't pretend to know what you go through as a black man. You sure haven't explained it to me. So when you come in here talking and you jump on my case because I wanna hear all of the facts before I make a decision then, we have a bigger problem. Maybe if you took the chip off your shoulder and realize that everyone is not out to get you, then maybe we can get somewhere.
(she walks away)

Terrell:
I am in the Twilight Zone.

LIKE A WHIRLWIND

(Knock on the door)
Daniel:
Who is it?

Rebecca:
It's Rebecca!

Daniel:
Rebecca? What's she doing here?

Rebecca:
Can you open the door? I need to talk to you.

Daniel:
Hey, um. What's up?

Rebecca:
Can I come in? Dag.

Daniel:
Uh sure. What brings you by?

Rebecca:
Look, I don't know how to say this so I'm gonna just say it. I'm HIV+

Daniel:
What?

Rebecca:
You heard me.

Daniel:
For how long?

Rebecca:
2 years.

Daniel:
Two years! Why are you telling me this now!

Rebecca:
I didn't find out until after us, Daniel.
I honestly didn't know how to tell you.

Daniel:
Did you get Daniel, Jr. checked?

Rebecca:
Yea, he's fine. Thank God.

Daniel:
For now, that stuff can lie dormant like 10 years!
I don't understand. How are you HIV+ but Daniel Jr isn't?

Rebecca:
I don't know-

Daniel:
Do I have it?!

Rebecca:
Well, have you been tested?

Daniel:
No Rebecca. It's not like I'm out here hoeing.

Rebecca:
Look. I am so sorry to spring this up on you. I was getting sick a lot, I thought it was stress. So I really didn't see a need to go to the doctor's. It got worse and worse when finally I decided to go.

Daniel:
This isn't making any sense. You were getting sick for 2 years and you didn't think to go to the hospital?

Rebecca:
Come on, Daniel. It wasn't consistently. And everyone is different.

Daniel:
Tell me about it. You had this before us, didn't you?

Rebecca:
It looks like it.

Daniel:
It looks like it. So you just came over here to ruin my life, again. It's bad enough we have a child together. NOW, you're telling me that there is a possibility that I maybe HIV +!
Is there anything else you wanna tell me?

Rebecca:
There is one more thing.

Daniel:
Oh great.

Rebecca:
This sickness is really taking its toll on me, you know because I wasn't taking any medication or anything. I'll be in the hospital a lot. DJ is gonna have to live with you.

Daniel:
(Death stare)
When?

Rebecca:
As soon as possible. I'm being admitted Monday.

Daniel:
And today's Saturday.

Rebecca:
Come on Daniel, I really need you to step up.

Daniel:
Step up? Step up?! I needed you to step up and be responsible but clearly that hasn't worked out has it? You expect to come in here disrupt my life because you didn't take care of yourself. Now, I'm a

full time Dad and who could possibly be HIV+. You destroy lives wherever you go.

Rebecca:
I'm sorry, Daniel. I really am. I call you when I bring DJ.

Daniel:
Sigh.

GAMES ARE TOO STRONG

Leo:
When my love is gone. It's gone
No trying to come back and make it work.
Especially when I knew your worth.
I stayed in your game while you took your time to finally comply.
That who I am, is who I am.
I had to be patient and watch you scrutinize everything I did because
the jokers you previously picked wore you out.
So now you can't tell if the real one is a real one because I'm a man of my word.
I don't keep you guessing cause I'm the true blessing
That you still can't see.
You expect me to bleed from your words and pretend that they don't hurt.
All because of the men who didn't see your worth.
Tired of trying, tired of bombing.
When organized chaos is your normal
Peace doesn't exist.
Too many hurt women look for men to heal them
When we gotta heal ourselves.
But because we're men, that's what we're supposed to do.

Alicia:
I never said I didn't love you. I never said I wasn't true.
There were just too many good things that I couldn't believe it was really you.
Heart-broken I have been
Torn apart since when,
I can remember asking will this ever end?
Then you came and I wasn't ready but I knew I desired something steady.
Wanting to show the real me but also really scared for you to see the real me.
Tough as I claim with a bloody heart I blame
Giving the benefit of the doubt because I was too ashamed
To remain, single.
Putting band aids on wounds that never properly healed.
That showed itself whenever you were near.

I'm sorry, is probably too late
But I hope we win.
Cause you're the only one I can see within.

Leo:
Wishful hearts and sweet replies
Is how you won.
Unfortunately for you,
I am the wrong one.
There's so much one can take
A beating at the stake
For love, why?
The risk is misplaced.
Adult love can be true love if both parties are ready.
But running after you has become too heavy.
One day you're up, next day you're down.
I'm everything to you but for me never a sound.
The imbalance that we dwell can never repair the whole in heart that others
Freely wear.
Maybe not me but the next man will see
The diamond in the ground you hide from me.

Alicia:
My love, my love
Draw near next to me. It is you I desire
Without any fear.
Another chance I ask
To show you my best.
It's you that I love, to that I can attest.
Love is not a battlefield but a life of sweet bliss
That I'd love to share with every sweet kiss.
Your heart are my thoughts that burn and tear
The insecurities and strife that
Swarms my ear.
I open to you
In hopes it'll lead
The breaths of life
Of you to me.

MAN OF THE HOUSE

Brian:
Who is Damon?

Regina:
Well hello to you too.

Brian:
Not today, Regina. Who is Damon?

Regina:
Just a teacher that I work with. What is your problem?

Brian:
My problem is these texts that I keep getting.
Oh, you took the wrong phone.

Regina:
Brian, it's nothing. He's harmless. Honestly.
Nothing you need to worry over.

Brian:
You mean the text, "I can't wait to take you away from this."
You mean harmless like that?

Regina:
He's a flirt. Ok. It's really not that serious. I come home to you right?
Why are you worrying?

Brian:
Because you don't see this man flirting as a problem.
I don't give you enough affection?

Regina:
You give me everything that I need. I'm not cheating, if that's what you're thinking.
You know that school has about 5 black teachers.

Brian:
He's being disrespectful and your allowing it.

Regina:
Oh, how the table have turned. Where was all this when Lisa was flirting with you huh?
And that heifer had the audacity to try it in front of my face!
And what did you do?
"Regina, I don't know what she' doing."
Brian:
It's completely different. I don't talk to Lisa on the phone. I'm not telling her what he's telling you.

Regina:
You know this double standard that you have is mind boggling. A woman will flirt with you, somehow, you're just clueless. But you sure don't tell them to stop. What do you do? "Regina you're being paranoid" And you mean to tell me that this man showing me attention is so disrespectful that it has you walking up in here like you're about to blow this house down.

Brian:
Ahaha! So you admit, you like this attention.

Regina:
I never said I didn't. You mean to tell me you don't like it when Lisa was acting she could take her hands off of you?

Brian:
Ok, she no longer does that.

Regina:
How do I know?

Brian:
You don't trust me?

Regina:
Why should I? It's not like you've made any effort to make our relationship any better.

Brian:
I bought you a car.

Regina:
With my money.

Brian:
We moved into a bigger house.

Regina:
Again, with my money. See, what you fail to realize is that every upgrade that we have done recently was with my money. You might as well be the house husband.

Brian:
I have a business to run.

Regina:
Is that what you call it? Oh, that's adorable. For the past three years, I've made more money than you. Been more successful than you. Been taken more serious than you.
I'm actually better than you. Honestly, where would you be if I would have left?
You worried about Damon when you should be worrying about making
this relationship work.

Brian:
Where is this coming from? When I was making all the money. I paid for your college tuition so you didn't have to work. Your car note and insurance. All you had to do was drive. Weren't you the one that said Brian, go ahead and start your business. I can hold us done until it makes a profit?

Regina:
Keyword. PROFIT. We're still waiting on a profit. And if you really expected me to hold us down without you contributing anything, you are sadly mistaken. I'm tired of doing your job. If you can't provide monetarily the least you can do provide in other ways.
I thought you would have gotten a job or something.

Brian:
Wow, so when did being the provider mean you could do whatever you want.

Regina:
Since I became the man.
You don't like it? Make some money.

I SEE YOU LOUD AND CLEAR

Lamar:
Amani. How was school today?

Amani:
It was ok. Classes were boring as usual.

Lamar:
Your teacher called.

Amani:
Which one?

Lamar:
Spanish.

Amani:
Ugh, I didn't do anything.

Lamar:
She didn't say you did. She actually said that you were one of her brightest students. She was concerned for you. One of the boys in your class was harassing you.

Amani:
Not harassing. Just being annoying. Nothing I can't handle.

Lamar:
She said it was pretty bad.

Amani:
It was but I handled it. He called me a burnt cabbage patch baby and I called him a 30-day old turd.

Lamar:
Um, why?

Amani:
Why did I call him a 30-day old turd?

Lamar:
No, why did he call you a burnt cabbage patch.

Amani:
Because they were going around the class saying that lighter girls were prettier and I wasn't having it.

Lamar:
What did he say to you?

Amani:
He told me that I was too dark for any boy to want to be with me. They can barely see me.

Lamar:
How does that make you feel?

Amani:
It makes me feel like nothing. That little boy doesn't faze me.

Lamar:
Do you believe what he says?

Amani:
What? That lighter skin girls are prettier? Do you believe that, Daddy?

Lamar:
Do I believe what?

Amani:
Lighter skin is prettier.

Lamar:
All black women are beautiful.

Amani:
Well, why are the women you date either light skin or Latino? I have never seen you with a dark-skinned woman.

Lamar:
It's just my preference.

Amani:
So your preference says lighter is prettier. Matter of fact, the only dark-skinned woman I've seen you with is mom.

Lamar:
This is not about me, Mani. It's about you.

Amani:
Yea ok. You miss her?

Lamar:
Who, your mother?

Amani:
Duh? Who else would I be talking about?

Lamar:
I hope that she's doing well, wherever she is. You're not mad at her for leaving us?

Amani:
No. She left you. You're the one who cheated…with your "preference"
Such a typical athlete. HA! So no, I ain't mad at her.

Lamar:
Well, no lighter isn't better. All are equally beautiful.

Amani:
Hmm mm. You don't have to try and convince me that you don't miss mom.

Lamar:
Where is this coming from?

Amani:
You act like I don't see you staring at her picture that is STILL on the counter.

Lamar:
It's a photo of you too.

Amani:
Daddy you have plenty photos of me. So miss me with that. But go ahead. Act like you don't want her back. While you look miserable dating these whatevers that won't ever measure up to mom. Love Ya!

Lamar:
Laughs. Walks over to the photo and sighs.
She sounds just like her mother.

FINISH WHAT YOU STARTED

Malcolm:
There's so much I want to say to you but I can't.

Tracy:
You can't. You have a girlfriend, remember?

Malcolm:
It's long distance and it's not working out.

Tracy:
That's exactly why you need to keep your mouth shut.

Malcolm:
I knew I should have picked you from the beginning.

Tracy:
Shut up Malcolm.

Malcolm:
Trina is a lot. She's always going here, there. She won't stay put for longer than 6 months.

Tracy:
She's a free spirit, you knew that when you got with her. You thought you were gonna change that? OK.

Malcolm:
Not change it but calm it down a bit. First, she's in Atlanta. Next, she's in New York then Toronto. Who knows where she'll be next! At least you're predictable. I know where you'll be.

Tracy:
Excuse me? That's not a compliment.

Malcolm:
What I meant is that you're stable.

Tracy:
Stable because I don't travel? I travel. It may not be as much as Trina but I travel.

Malcolm:
I didn't mean it like that. She' just a lot to handle. I'm looking for something simpler.

Tracy:
You mean less challenging.

Malcolm:
Yes, I mean noooo. Look. Everything I say is going to sound like a dig to you. It' not supposed to.

Tracy:
I think you need to figure out what you want.
I may not be as adventurous or challenging as Trina but I do have a side.

Malcolm:
I know, I know. I like your side.

Tracy:
Do you even know what my side is?

Malcolm:
It's different than Trina's.

Tracy:
Really?

Malcolm:
I mean, hey. Ok. You are very different from her. We hang out a whole lot more than I did when Trina was here. Yes, Trina is a free spirit but we no longer gel.

Tracy:
How did you know you don't? You've given up on her and she's not even here.
And you're trying to include me?! No Malcolm. This is all wrong.

Malcolm:
Are you saying you've NEVER felt the chemistry between us? I know I do, even now I do.

Tracy:
Well, you need to unfeel it. Trina is a close friend of mine and I'm not doing that to her.

Malcolm:
What about you? Don't you think you deserve happiness?

Tracy:
Why couldn't you finish whatever you and Trina had before coming to me?!
Now, this looks like some unnecessary sneaky mess that can ruin my friendship and I'm not losing her for you. My friendship means everything even if it doesn't mean anything to you.

Malcolm:
Ok, Tracy. Don't answer this right away just think about it. Would Trina do the same for you if the shoe was on her foot?

Tracy:
Your timing absolutely sucks, Malcolm.
Regardless of what she would or wouldn't do, it doesn't excuse you trying to begin something with me and you're still dating my friend. That's a mess.

THE CULPRIT

Raine:
Sometimes we lie because the truth is just as bad. We think we're being righteous when in fact we're only thinking of ourselves. You walk around here like nothing can touch you. Like nothing affects you. Do you still feel that same way?

Mark:
Please. I don't know you.

Raine:
But you know her…and her…and her. Look familiar? No? Let me help you. This one, killed in a car crash. Her strangled to death. And her, throat slit and thrown in the river.

Mark:
I don't know who you think I am but I can promise you, YOU HAVE THE WRONG PERSON!

Raine:
Haha, I can see why they fell for you. Good looking, charming, "seems" sincere.

Mark:
I don't know these women, I've never seen them, never talked to them.

Raine:
Ok, Ok. Well if you don't know them, you wanna tell me why we found a secret phone that somehow has their numbers?

Mark:
I don't know! I don't have a secret phone. Did you check my assistant? I only have 2 phones. One phone I keep and the other phone she keeps?!

Raine:
Oh, Marky Mark and the funky bunch. Give up the act. I've got you. You see, the last detective was on your payroll so they quietly put

these to bed. Unfortunately for you, you can't afford me. So I did my job…and then some. Apparently, you got a little cocky. Meeting the friends, the parents. Never being seen in public but still allowing the public to see you. They all described you! (Laughs.) And to make matters worse, they have pictures of you. I don't know if you the dumbest murderer or what!

Mark:
Look officer-

Raine:
No you look. If you don't confess right now, I'll be forced to show you what I really have…Marcellus.
Mark:
What?!

Raine:
I told you. You can't afford me. Marcellus Brown of Canton OH. Star athlete, abusive mother. Poor home life, unsolved murder should I go on?

Mark:
So, you did your homework. There's nothing there.

Raine:
I took the liberty of getting that little case unsealed. It seems you and mommy had a falling out, huh? Never came to your games, never supported you and even cheated on your weak father. So you decided not to get over that rejection. You didn't give those women a choice to like your mother did.

Mark:
They all deserved it. You should be thanking me. No one will miss them.

Raine:
Well thank you Ranger Bob. For ridding us of the cold- hearted women. It is not your right or obligation. That's what we have law enforcement for.

Mark:
Well law enforcement didn't know what they were doing. They would have private parties humiliating men. Making them crawl on all fours, eat dog food. Treating them like animals. Dogs. All because these men played them.

Raine:
How did you find out about this?

Mark:
My assistant. She was at a club. That's how they recruit.

Raine:
Where are these private parties?

Mark:
Uh uh, what am I getting out of this?

Raine:
The chance to stop them. THE RIGHT WAY.

Mark:
You think I'm gonna give you more information without-I WANT FULL IMMUNITY.

Raine:
Guard! I don't have time for this.

Mark:
I'm the only one that knows what's going on. You don't even where to start first. You have a choice. Full immunity and you get all of the information or I get nothing so you get nothing. What's it gonna be? DETECTIVE.

WHAT ABOUT ME?

Taylor:
The baby's crying.

Dan:
Are you gonna get her?

Taylor:
Can you? I haven't had any sleep all day.

Dan:
I have an important meeting in an hour.

Taylor:
Fine.

Dan:
Thank you.

Taylor:
Heifer.

Dan checks his phone and gets right up.

Taylor:
I thought you said in an hour?

Dan:
They moved it up.

Taylor:
To 7?

Dan:
Taylor, it's my job. What is wrong with you.

Taylor:
What is wrong with me? Maybe it's because you roll over and jump EVERYTIME you job calls you. I would sure like that kind of attention.

Dan:
Here we go again.

Taylor:
Yes, here we go again.

Dan:
You had no problem with me working any hours I needed when you were working. Are you bored Taylor taking care of our baby? Do you want a real job?

Taylor:
First of all, I didn't even want children. YOU wanted it.
What did you say? A child will complete our family and bring us closer. Trust you.
HA! Trust you!
I sure didn't trust you to bring another woman into this marriage, did I?

Dan:
But our child did bring us together. We live as a family more. It's not just me and you going to work. We might as well be single or in a relationship. Having children is what married people do. And I told you, she's not a problem anymore. It was one mistake.

Taylor:
Then why is she telling you to come to work an hour early? You really think I'm gonna believe that whatever meeting at 8am is so important that she had to have you come an hour early? That one mistake Dan was for 3 months. So, don't insult my intelligence trying to downplay it.

Dan:
Look, I have all I want right here. You don't need to feel insecure about her anymore.

Taylor:
I'm not insecure about her. I don't know who I am anymore. I'm just your wife and Danielle's mother. When we got together, I was on the verge of becoming partner at my firm. And that was 5 years ago. Now look at me. I'm not practicing law or anything.

Dan:
It's that what you wanted? Someone who could take care of you? So you didn't have to?

Taylor:
No. I wanted someone I could work with and build. It just seems like I don't have any dreams anymore. Like this is my life, forever. You don't think I don't want to go back to work? Of course I do. I miss it every day. You don't care that I feel trapped?

Dan:
How about this. When the baby reaches one, we'll talk about starting you back part time?
Truce?

Taylor:
I'll write a contract. Have a good day.

Dan:
I told you about calling my house in the morning, she's suspecting us again.
Yes, that's a bad thing!
I still have to come home to her, you don't.
Just give me more time. She wants to start working again. Once that happens, she won't care what I'm doing. And you'll have my full attention. You have to be patient.

RELIGIOUS SECRETS

Rick:
What is this?

Karla:
Hey babe, what are you talking about?

Rick:
This letter, from a girl named Shantel.

Karla:
Rick, I don't know a Shantel.

Rick:
Well she knows you. She says she'd your daughter.

Karla:
This is a prank, right?

Rick:
Do I look like I'm playing?

Karla:
I don't have a daughter.

Rick
According to this letter you do.

Karla:
My what?
(reads the letter)
I-how did you find this?

Rick:
I didn't find anything, she came to the door.
When were you gonna tell me you had a daughter?

Karla:
Rick, that was a long time ago. I was very young-

Rick:
So this is why you didn't want children. Because you already had one!
You didn't like children. I sat there and took it like a champ and loved you anyway.
When all along, you had this secret.

Karla:
It was a part of my past that I-

Rick:
Didn't feel the need to share. When are you going to be completely honest?
For better or worse, right? I'm finding out so much about you that it makes me wonder why I married you? A daughter Karla?

Karla:
Look, I was in high school. It was a very dark time in my life. I had no one to turn to.

Rick:
Don't give me your round the way explanation. I'm getting tired of these pop truths you're keep giving me.

Karla:
I don't want you to feel sorry for me, I've moved on.

Rick:
Karla, you have a 14-year-old daughter. I want the truth!

Karla:
Fine. I was 16 in high school and I was raped by my Math teacher. Happy?!

Rick:
I thought you went to some preppy Christian School?

Karla:
And you think that makes it any better? They were more concerned about the backlash of their reputation than one of their students. They manipulated me and my mom so bad that we didn't press charges and gave up my baby for adoption. What did I get in return? A full ride to college and enough hush money to last me all 4 years. So, do you really think I want to relive that part of my life? No, I'd like to forget about it. The pain, the embarrassment, the regret of letting people tell me what to do with my body and my baby. I literally had no voice. I try to block that out of my mind as much as possible.

Rick:
Karla, I'm sorry you went through that-

Karla:
No, Rick. I don't need sympathy, I don't! I'm better off anyway. I mean look at me, I'm beautiful. I have my own successful business, a man that truly loves me. I have all that I hope or dream. I don't care about them! They can all rot in hell if you ask me!
Yea, I showed 'em!

(Rick hugs her while she's crying)
Rick:
I'm here.

Karla:
Why me? Why?

Rick:
I know.

Karla:
I'm tired Rick. Just tired.

HIDDEN LOVE, THAT'S TRUE

Mina:
Hello? Oh my gosh. Thank you for telling me. I'll let him know immediately.

Jackson:
Hey.

Mina:
Hey. Sit down for a second.

Jackson:
What's wrong?

Mina:
The hospital called. Your mother passed away in her sleep last night.

Jackson:
Ok.

Mina:
Ok?

Jackson:
Thank you for telling me.

Mina:
Are you going to call your brother and sister?

Jackson:
Sometime today.

Mina:
Ok, maybe you should take some time to process this.

Jackson:
I'm fine, Mina. Those two haven't lifted finger to help me with mom. But she loved them the most. Nothing they could do was ever wrong in her sight.

She loved them like they were her only children and I was after thought.

Mina:
Jackson, your mom used to tell me all the time that she loved you.

Jackson:
Well she had a funny way of telling me. Do this, do that. That's not good enough. You need to step up, you're the oldest. They need a role model. Be better for them. Watch over them. When she needed all of us the most? Who was there? ME!

Mina:
I'm sure she knows her kids. Give her some credit. She did raise you guys.

Jackson:
I can't stand those two. Now that mom died, they're gonna come around like they've been doing all of the work without me.

Mina:
At the end of the day babe, you and your mother knew the truth.

Jackson:
My mother?

Mina:
She left a letter for you.
I'll read it.
Dear Jackson, oh how you have grown to be a wonderful man. I'd like to think I had a hand in that but it was your father that brought out the genuine person that you are. Take care of your brother and sister, they're helpless without. Don't be upset because they didn't come to see me a lot. I'm not. I knew who would step up and who wouldn't. You were always the strongest, most loyal and loving of you 3 and I want you to know, I have ALWAYS loved you. You actually were my favorite. All of my affairs are in order, so there's no need to try and fix or change it. The company will go to your sister and brother because I know you have no interest in working there. So, for you my boy when you go to the reading of my will, you

will get a key. That key will forever be the key to my heart that you had when I first laid eyes on you so long ago. It is also a key to a downtown building that is completely yours to open that restaurant you have always wanted. Go to AT Credit Union, you will find a joint savings account between you and I only. After my death, the account is solely yours. Let's just say you have enough money to live off for the rest of your life…without working. Live your dreams Jackson, they are there for a reason. Your first priority is to yourself and then to Mina. Cherish her and love her unconditionally. You're not gonna find any better. I have always loved you. Always believed in you. My first born, My giant.

Love Mom.

Jackson:
I had her all wrong.

Mina:
Most of the time, we always do.

LOVE OF DRAMA

Sam:
What are we doing here?

Alana:
What are you talking about?

Sam:
I'm just tired, Alana.

Alana:
Tired of what?

Sam
Of…this!

Alana:
Sam, where is this coming from? I just walked in the door!

Sam:
We say the same thing, eat the same thing, do the same thing.
You're not bored?

Alana:
Bored? I love our life. We have good jobs. We love each other. Built
a great home.
What more do you want?

Sam:
If you have to ask then…we have a bigger problem.

Alana:
Sam, I am so confused. I just talk to you on the phone 10 minute ago.
I asked you-

(In Unison)
Sam and Alana:
What do you want for dinner cause I don't feel like cooking.

Sam:
But what do you do? Cook. Why? Because that's what you do!

Alana:
Ok. Stop talking. Sit down, take a break.
Speak to me in full sentences.
What is wrong with you?

Sam:
You know I love you right?

Alana:
Without a doubt.

Sam:
How do you know you'll love me in a year?

Alana:
Because I'm choosing to love you.

Sam:
But how do you know it'll be the same later on?

Alana:
Because I am who I am. I'm not changing.

Sam:
You don't see nothing wrong with that? You not changing?

Alana:
Sam, am I supposed to change? Am I supposed to be different?

Sam:
YES! You're supposed to want to grow, see and learn new things. Be spontaneous every once in a while. I'm just tired of being bored.

Alana:
Bored of who? ME?
You're bored with me?
When did this start? I've always been who I was simple and content.

Now, all of a sudden you have a problem with that? This is who you married!
You knew that and NOW you're bored? What do you expect me to do? Jump out of who I am to appease whatever mid-life crisis you're going through? I've never asked you to change for me. I've accepted that you're over dramatic and loud. That you just won't throw your dirty clothes in the hamper WHEN ITS RIGHT NEXT TO THE DOOR or when you see me cleaning the LAST thing you would do is HELP. Or, my favorite one, when everything is going find and peaceful, you decide to make some God forsaken war cry about you need some excitement in your life.
Well you know what. GO! You're tired? I'm tired. Tired of going through this with you every single leap year. Love and Marriage is not something you fall into. It is a choice. A choice that you fervently make that come hell or high water, I'm gonna be here. If you can no longer make that commitment? Then we need to think otherwise.
(Starts walk away, talking to herself)
Bored of me? Who does he think he is?!

Sam:
Alana, I love you.

Alana:
Sigh. Rolls her eyes.

YOU THINK YOU WANT THIS

Monroe:
Hey.

Rachel:
Hey.

Monroe:
Did you read my letter?

Rachel:
Yea.

Monroe:
And?

Rachel:
And what?

Monroe:
Come on Rachel, do you want me to spell it out?

Rachel:
Are you serious about this letter?

Monroe:
No doubt.

Rachel:
Well…

Monroe:
I messed up. I lied to you. Played games with you and I apologize. We were in college, talking about how we were going to take over the world together. Stayed all night making plans that I honestly knew I would never do. I sat and watched you tell me what your goals and because I didn't think I could handle or was jealous I sabotaged our future life together. I miss you, Rachel. I should have never done that to you

Rachel:
Thank you for your apology. 5 years late but no less an apology. I want to tell you what your immature actions did to me. Since you left. I almost didn't graduate because I was physically ill and couldn't go to class. Like I was really going to tell the wellness center that I was sick from a broken heart and they'd believe me. I was depressed for 4 weeks. Racking my brain, going over our ENTIRE relationship trying to figure what I did wrong. What you don't realize in leaving is how the other person will take it. You don't even know who heart-broken I was. Crying EVERY night. Barely getting out a bed. Wanting to talk to you, wanting to kill you, needing to hold you, thinking about strangling you. It all became one messy mental breakdown, because of you. You're lack honesty nearly cost me my life because I couldn't understand how could someone claim to love me...all of me and still drop me off a cliff.

Monroe:
I understand.

Rachel:
You don't.

Monroe:
But, I do. I soon found out that me trying to take the easier road was actually worse.
She was nothing like you. Didn't have the same drive, didn't have your authenticity. She complained too much. Never saw the positive side. I tried talking to her about the things I wanted to do and all in all, it just became about her. I wasn't inspired with her. I actually preferred not talking to her. Everything I thought she was, a lie. She pretended to like everything I did just to get into a relationship. I was trapped. Then tells me she wants a baby. I tried to leave but she would hurt herself. Telling me that I was her lifeline. That being with me gave her life meaning and she couldn't see herself without me. There were so many times I wanted to call you, to hear your voice, hear your laugh, ANYTHING. Because I was sinking in my own mess.

Rachel:
What do you expect me to do?
I don't know you anymore, I don't trust you.

Monroe:
Just think of me as a new person you're meeting.
I know I've messed up. If I know you, I know that you'd rather not even look at me. But if I don't try, I will always regret that I didn't step up and be the man I was supposed to be all that time.

Rachel:
And see, that's where you need to rethink. Who said that I WANT you here. You may be a new person and I commend you for that, but what if I don't want you at all?
I'm so sick of men not knowing what's in front of them WHEN it's in front of them.
Why do you have to go through chaos to see that paradise was right where you left it.
I know that I wasn't the outgoing type, didn't have the clothes or popularity that you needed to feel secure in your pick. You chose the outer appearance and left me to pick up the pieces.
You think I could trust someone like that again? To freely put my heart back into that's person's hands knowing that there is a strong possibility that we could repeat the same cycle? You're crazy. Just like you grew, so did I. I'm not sure I can do that.

Sam:
Sometimes we have to learn because we're stupid. Impatient and insecure. I had a lot of growing to do. You've always had my heart. Even when I was with her, I thought about you, constantly. That's when I knew it was you.

Rachel:
While you were thinking of me. I was searching. Alone.
But I needed that. I would have never found out who I was. To be strong and confident.
I've learned that I don't need you. To be frank, I don't want you. The person I was back then is gone.
You say you've changed, and that's great! Don't you think I would've changed too?

**Ask yourself, would you even like who I am now?
It would be a shame if you were trying to rekindle a college love with
a grown woman.**

LOVERS OVER FRIENDS

Keith:
We have been friends for what 10 years?
You didn't mind hearing about all the women I dealt with. What changed?
Oh yea, you found love in hopeless place.
B, it's tired.
This is the same dude that had y'all go Dutch on your first date.
Makes plans then changes them at the last minute and rarely says sorry.
Who do you wind up hanging with? ME.
But I'm the disrespectful one.

Bebe:
Keith, you're being over dramatic. He's extremely nice. Educated. You know he's a doctor so things happen at the drop of a hat.

Keith:
He's a gynecologist!! What could possibly be an emergency? Dried up- you know what I'm not even going there.

Bebe:
Ok fine. He's getting better.

Keith:
Why are you settling for someone that has to? I can't stand women who claim to be so independent and bout it but as soon you get a man comes in, y'all turn soft and let him get away with crap you wouldn't even let your friends get away with.

Bebe:
Ok, that's not the point.

Keith:
Oh, I'm not finished. Then dude gets mad at me like I'm the problem. Saying you don't need to be around me because there's some underlying feelings.
Nah bro. I can see past your bull.

Bebe:
Fine. It doesn't compare to the raggedy girls I hear from you.

Keith:
Oh God.

Bebe:
How many pregnancy scares have you had? Huh? Huh?

Keith:
3.

Bebe:
Yea, in 3 months by 3 different women. You have yet to bring someone that's even on your ex-fiancé's level.

Keith:
Alright man, there is no need to bring her up.

Bebe:
I do. Because ever since she left, I don't know who you are. You've never been this player type. Talking to 3 different women at the same time. You are out here LITERALLY acting up.

Keith:
Ummm we're not talking about me.

Bebe:
We are now.

Keith:
The point I'm making is this. We both are jacked up. And we gotta do better. We're almost 40.

Bebe:
Yea I know. But men are annoying!

Keith:
So are you!

Do you know how irritating it is to hear I'm fabulous I don't need a man to I love me…over and over and over.

Bebe:
Ok, ok. Calm down. We need to figure this out. I'm not growing old with you.
Unmarried or with no kids.

Keith:
Yea, not gonna lie. I do want kids.

Bebe and Keith:
Ughhhh.

PURSUE AND GET WHAT IS YOURS...YOUR SANITY DEPENDS ON IT

www.ingramcontent.com/pod-product-compliance
Lightning Source LLC
Chambersburg PA
CBHW081357290426
44110CB00018B/2401